Letting Go

One Golfer's Journey

Roger Douglas

Revision 1

Dedication

To Tino Salgado, my friend, my barber, and my
coach, who listens patiently to my tales of the golf
journey every month.

Alice said to herself rather sharply, "I advise you to leave off this minute." She generally gave herself good advice. (though she very rarely followed it.)

Alice in Wonderland

Table of Contents

Introduction

Most books on golf are written by professional golfers, teachers or tour players. These writers have helpful tips, drills, and other information to improve the game. Usually they are filled with anecdotes from some of the great tour players, all of which I fit in a category, called top down. This book comes from the bottom up. It is not written by an expert, not even by a particularly good golfer. I was going to give the book the title: "I'll shoot my age, if I have to live to 105." Unfortunately, Bob Hope had already used that line. The primary purpose of this endeavor is not to lower your golf score. This may happen. If so, it comes as a secondary benefit. My mission for this book is to change how one relates fundamentally to the game.

If you are a low handicapper, the one who looks forward to the club championship, then this book may not be for you. My task is to transform the reader's experience on the golf course so that it becomes more enjoyable. In order for this to happen, I would hope to eliminate some of the frustration and distress that seems endemic to many average golfers.

Five years ago I started to play golf. I am only slightly past the beginning stage. I have taken lessons, sent for equipment, spent time on the internet, and on the practice range, much of it with little return. Inadvertently, I have found some valuable lessons outside the commonplace instructions. Golf can be a difficult game to master, but it can also be a rich source for learning about life.

Graham Green, the well known English novelist, theorized that writing is a form of therapy. This certainly has been my experience. What has become abundantly clear to me is that golf brings to light many of life's issues that rarely surface except perhaps around two AM on a sleepless night. Golf is therapy in the deepest sense of the word. Golf teaches us about our fragility, need for forgiveness, and the possibility of healing. I set out to teach myself how to play the game and found that I had opened myself to some of life's basic questions--issues that could be raised on a psychiatrist's couch more easily then on a golf course.

For some golfers, the temptation is to view golf as a game to fill in the blank spaces of our busy lives. For others, golf is a social experience that allows some modicum of exercise in a sedentary existence. But golf can also be a doorway into deeper truths wherein we can discover new understandings of a sport that has intrigued people for over 500 years.

My motivation for writing about the golf experience was that I found myself puzzled by the contradictions inherent in the game. The more I tried to improve, the worse I seemed to play. The more I immersed myself in lessons, advice from magazines, tips from my fellow players, the less I seemed to enjoy the game. Golf became both a burden and an addiction. It was at that point that I realized a need to view golf with a different set of eyes. For me, writing has always served as a way to discover new insights. It is an opportunity to sort out all the information that is readily available from books and the internet.

At the outset, I viewed golf as a problem to be solved. It could be mastered in a year or two as long as I worked hard, practiced interminably and added a strong dose of determination. This problem solving approach had worked through out my life. It was only when I began thinking of golf as a mystery not to be solved but to be embraced, that new understandings emerged. When I played the game with this in mind, I was able to accept that one could never predict what would happen from one day to the next. Golf, like life itself, had a perverse refusal to be packaged, managed, or even predicted.

Is it possible to play the game without depending upon solutions to obvious problems? Could one move from easy answers to taking into account many unknown options? In order to play in this mode, you have to accept initially that much of life is not under your control. Somehow I had to learn to free myself from the constraints of the past. Then I had to put aside the temptation of projecting a negative future. The process of letting go and not anticipating was one of the early learnings.

Most instructional manuals readily admit that golf is played more in your mind than in your body. Bobby Jones, one of the original golf instructors, wrote: "Golf is a game played on a five inch course, the distance between your ears." The amazing thing is that in most golf books little emphasis is given to preparation of the mind. Some writers simply advise golfers to keep the mind a blank or to learn to cultivate a positive attitude. Somehow this reminds me of the advice to keep smiling even as your life goes to pieces. This is not to denigrate some thoughtful writers. They, in their own way, attempt to be helpful , though little emphasis is given to the mind. Most books feature the body mechanics with no more then a passing reference to the thought process which strongly influences the game.

Even the most rank amateur knows that both conscious and unconscious factors are major parts of the golf swing. It is the writer's contention that the mind, or to be more specific, our thoughts can be controlled. Just as you can increase your strength by exercising your muscles through practice at a gym, so too can you get better at golf by exercising certain parts of your mind. The mind is a critical factor in playing good golf. Therefore is it any wonder that some sort of mind training will be mentioned. Mind training promises to boost our ability to focus on the present moment.

I am indebted to two very different people as I write. I am sure that each would be amazed that he is mentioned in a book about golf. One is a psychiatrist by the name of Dr. Milton Erickson, and the other is a Roman Catholic Priest, Fr. Richard Rohr.

Dr. Erickson has written extensively about motivation and the place of the unconscious in healing. Unlike Freud, he believed the unconscious mind did not consist of unsavory forces. His writings with the use of stories demonstrate how the unconscious was a source of wisdom and could be used to navigate difficult circumstances. I have freely borrowed from him and others to underscore many of the salient points of this new way to play the game.

The second author is the Rev. Richard Rohr, a Franciscan priest, who has writen on spirituality and the inner life. One of his recurrent themes is that in the first half of life, we are driven by a need for success and self identity. Most of what we do is motivated by a wish to become better in any enterprise in which we are involved. In the second half of life he raises another question. The critical issue for Rohr is: Can I find meaning in a life characterized by loss and failure?

For me, golf is a second half of life game. I can only imagine that neither Erickson nor Rohr has ever swung a golf club. Each, in his own way, has taught me to deal with the game. I learned at an early stage that golf is a game characterized by mistakes. We hold in high regard those golfers who fail less often. We know also that there is no such thing as a flawless round of play. One way we learn is by making fewer mistakes and solving recurring problems as suggested by the experts. Another way is by learning to live with imperfection, trusting the unconscious, and discovering valuable lessons of life in a relatively simple game.

From time to time, I have used what some might label a Zen approach. I do not apologize for using this direction for it is the same as used by many of the great wisdom teachers. There seems to be a consensus in Zen that you have to search internally and not look for easy answers on the outside. The basic tools for growth lie inside ourselves.

Here is a typical Zen story type which is illustrative of the approach that I follow:

"A student asked a teacher, "What is the true way to play golf?" The teacher answered, "every way is the true way." To which the student replied, "Can I study it?" The teacher sat quietly and then responded: "The more you study it, the further you will be from the way."

Now the confused student asked, "But if I don't study it, how can I know it?" The teacher said, "The way does not belong to things seen, nor copied. Do not seek it, or name it. To find yourself on the way, open yourself and go internally."

Two things are important in this adjusted mini-satori. There are no easy answers given, and the student has to become his own teacher.

As I began to write I realized that I was exploring a subject about which I knew very little. It was as foreign to me as baseball would be to a British person. I could neither speak as an expert, nor a professional, not even as a seasoned player.

I felt more like a child making discoveries in some

far-off land. This started my thinking about children's books which were written in metaphoric language to help a child understand life's truths.

In turn, this led me to re-read Lewis Carroll's famous *Alice in Wonderland* which has the capacity to transport a child into a journey of amazing adventures and wondrous surprises. I have borrowed selective passages from Alice's odyssey to use as an ongoing metaphor for the game of golf.

Just as Carroll teaches us that life is a mixture of misery and mystery, miracles and marvels. So too can we discover that golf can contains fundamental truths about the journey through life.

I invite you now to join me on an internal voyage of a below average golfer and see if you can identify with some of the pitfalls that happen on a golfer's odyssey.

Let me start with a question, a question that will underlie much of what is being presented. Here is what I have asked myself as I set out to discover something of the game of golf beyond the golf game. What is it about the game of golf that makes it a fun experience?

Except for the infrequent times where I thoroughly won over an overbearing opponent. I confess that there is little about my past experiences on the golf course that I would place in the fun category. Indeed it was good exercise. (I probably could have gotten more from a regular trip to the gym.) And surely it enabled me to meet new people. (Probably could have found other less expensive venues for socializing.) And then it allowed me to gain some new skills. (Probably could also have learned new skills by taking up bowling.) So what was it that kept me appearing at the golf course three or four times a week? They say the definition of insanity is doing the same thing over and over again while expecting a different outcome. Much of what we call golf is craziness in the making. So join me on this journey, as we start with Louis Carrol's words:

There is a place like no other place on earth. A land full of wisdom, mystery, and danger. Some say to survive it you need to be mad as a hatter.

Do you think he was referring to the golf course?

Chapter One: In the Locker Room

"And so we shall begin at the beginning," the king said gravely, "and go on till you come to the end. Then stop."

The conversation is fairly routine as we put on our golf clothes and drink our second cup of coffee. We talk about the latest scores, how Phil or Tiger or Rory did this weekend, and a little local gossip. By the time we're tying our shoes, the many reasons why our game is not up to par can be heard. Our back has been hurting, our arthritis is kicking up, or we just haven't been playing. In this pre game ritual we are setting up excuses in advance.

My own particular conversation usually shares some new formula, new grip, or new way to swing. This, in effect, is another way of saying that this round of golf is an experiment, so don't be surprised if I do badly.

The locker room conversation, or the breakfast table talk all stem from the fear based parts of the mind, that part that anticipates trouble. We are preparing the way ahead of time. We anticipate a worse case scenario.

We announce our excuses in advance.

We know from past experiences that even when things seem to be going well, disaster can lurk just around the corner. Your drives may be booming, your approach shot is right on the green, and then you four putt from twelve feet out.

These negative thoughts are not limited to the pessimists among us. One of the marks of our common humanity is the ability to anticipate the future. This talent is probably what separates us from the rest of the animal world. It allows us to project into the future and to learn from the past. We say to ourselves, if we do as we did last week, we can imagine the result. This can be a two edged sword. It is a great aid to planning. At the same time it can mobilize anxiety.

To completely forget the past would be a great tragedy, but we can remember too much. We can be obsessed with the way it was and never glimpse how different our future could be. There is an old saying: "If you keep re-reading the past chapter you will never finish the book."

Here is where we realize the importance of cultivating our mental processes. Most times we do not do this. Our thoughts come to us in a hap hazard way. The Buddhists use the term *monkey mind* to describe our minds. This is in reference to the uncontrollable pattern of most of our thoughts. The mind seems to jump from one subject to another If we think about the subject at all we simply say that our mind has a mind of its own. If there is any shaping to be done, it is conditioned by past experiences.

One of the basic foundations of this book is that we can develop our minds by practice. The power to select certain thoughts and reject others is a skill to be developed. We do this by learning to focus, to concentrate, to be attentive. Then when we feel our minds straying, we learn to pull ourselves back to the present moment.

Many golf books have a section on the proper exercises to train your body for the vigorous game of golf. So do we have a need to exercise the mind. Our thoughts can be controlled. We may not be able to block negative thoughts, but we can turn a mindless mind into a mindful one. There are calisthenics for the mind as well as for the body.

On the way to the first Tee we stop off at the practice cage. We are there to warm up, but like most multitaskers we attempt to combine several jobs at once. Not only do we work out our stiffness, but we also try some drills we saw recently on YouTube. Combining tasks helps us to mis-hit many balls. I wonder why a bad practice signifies to many a bad game ahead. The practice Tee is not a rehearsal, it's a time to warm up our muscles. Suggested drills can be helpful, but not before going out to the first Tee.

Before we actually arrive at the first Tee, let me share one of my basic premises. I believe that all golfers have within themselves enough knowledge to play the game. It is not that we need to learn new things as much as it is that we need to be aware of what we are doing. Here is a story from Milton Erickson that points us in the direction as we begin this odyssey.

The story is about a horse that wandered into the family farm. No one knew who its owner was or where it belonged. Suggestions were given such as advertising in the local paper, calling everyone within a five mile radius, enlisting the animal safety people. Erickson said he knew how to find the owner. Let the horse tell us. And sure enough when allowed to go by itself with only a rope attached to keep it from wandering, the horse finally ended up at its home. The owner asked, "How did you know that the horse belonged to me?" Erikson said, "I didn't, but the horse knew."

The horse represents each one of us. We don't necessarily need outside support to find our way. What we need is self-awareness and possibly assistance to keep from wandering. This premise is why I am writing. It is my way of becoming more aware, of finding myself at home on the golf course, and of discovering new ways to enjoy the game

Chapter Two: On The First Tee

"This was not an encouraging opening for a conversation," Alice replied, rather shyly. "I -- I hardly know sir, just at present --at least I know who I was when I got up this morning, but I think I must have been changed several times since then." " "What do you mean by all that," said the Caterpillar sternly.

Why is it that many golfers report that the first hole is their least favorite? Once they complete the first hole, they often breathe a sigh of relief and say; "Now we can start."

As I waited to hit my first ball, at the beginning of my round, I became aware that similar to many golf clubs the dining area was directly in back of the first Tee. This allowed the breakfast crowd and or the lunch bunch to observe the golfers as they enjoyed their meal.

And then there were my fellow golfers, all standing, warming up, swinging their drivers and watching. I was also particularly aware of where the balls had landed from those who had teed off before me.

Standing in the Tee box, suddenly I'm overwhelmed by what I've labeled the "What ifs." What if the ball goes in the water? What if I miss hit and the ball lands in another fairway? What if I make a fool of myself? The choice of "the what ifs" is endless. But it is important to become aware of the reason these thoughts come to mind.

First, we might say what if it stems from the training to be problem solvers. In most of our ventures we try to anticipate failure. Prudent planning calls for heading off or at least identifying what could possibly go wrong. This may be a good strategy for problem solving, but it is not helpful on the first Tee. You do have an option. It is possible to step off the Tee box until these thoughts pass. You can acknowledge the "what ifs" and then go on to visualize a more successful conclusion. The ball goes straight for good yardage. The art of visualization can be cultivated. It is just as easy to say, "It is possible to hit the ball well rather than saying what if it lands in the water."

Second, we would have to admit these fears are instinctual. According to the neurobiologists, we have developed many more neurons that look for danger (problems to watch out for) then we have neurons that look for satisfaction. Fear-based thoughts are evident as far back as human history can recall. Fear was what enabled humankind to survive. Fear was a warning sign of danger ahead. Without fear many disasters could have happened. Fear-based responses are constantly on our minds. It can eat away at your game. Anybody with an ounce of imagination can easily call up one hundred ways that would spell failure as we get ready to hit the drive. As you stand on the Tee box, the big question is how to avoid succumbing to the underlying fears that threaten to ruin your swing.

Denial doesn't work. These fear fantasies have some basis in reality. We have flubbed shots in the past. Pretending they aren't present seems to make them stronger. What is pushed in the background often returns with renewed force.

The secret lies in learning to say "in spite of." In spite of the many fears, in spite of the many things that could go wrong, I will hit this drive the best way I can.

Saying "in spite of" takes a certain amount of courage. You have to be prepared to place fear where it belongs--as one factor among many other thoughts. Fears are real. They do not have to be as important as we tend to make them. Fear does not have to be the last word as we approach the opening drive.

The basic question is asking whether we control

our minds since we have a tendency to introduce a wide variety of unhelpful thoughts as we move onto the first tee. Here is a suggestion for the first practice exercise: Before you actually step on the T box, try to imagine your mind as a bottle of muddy water. The thoughts, the anxieties, the memories of past mistakes, the possibilities of future miss hits, are like the dirt that float around in the bottle of muddy water. Now, set the bottle down, refrain from stirring it, and surely enough the dirt will settle and the water will be clear. Then, and only then. step up to the tee.

The exercise does not suggest that the unhelpful thoughts will disappear, neither does the dirt. It reminds you that you are able to put aside those negatives. They no longer interfere with your game.

A second exercise that has helped from time to time was something I learned from the practice of meditation. When I feel fear coming on, I sometimes try to switch my attention to my breathing. I then begin to imagine my inhaling (breathing in) as taking in strength from the atmosphere, and then exhaling (breathing out) as a practice for letting go of those fears.

Finally, we might become aware of our motivational leanings. We are driven by a feelings of performance, particularly at the first hole. We are no longer the person who left our house. We are performers on a stage, and the audience is all around us. The important part of the game is whether this audience approves or disapproves of our play.

There are two basic things wrong here. One, when you focus on the audience you cannot keep the focus on the ball nor on the target. Two, when you focus on the performance, you're one step past hitting the ball. Your mind has jumped to whether the audience approves or disapproves of the drive. Performance anxiety takes away from concentration on the present moment. Any thought about the future or the past can seriously block being in the present moment.

Is it possible to get rid of these performance anxieties? Probably not. But you can lessen their power by understanding that the audience is probably more concerned with its own performance on the golf course. The first Tee anxiety is common to most golfers.

Chapter Three: The Bad Shot

Alice began to feel uneasy; to be sure, she had not as yet had any dispute with the queen. But she knew it might happen any minute, and then thought she, "what would become of me? They're dreadfully fond of beheading people here"

The next point of this odyssey comes during the fourth hole. I have lined up my pitching wedge, hoping to avoid the bunker and----that's right, my ball lands in the sand. But not just in the sand, it buries itself at a most awkward position. And I begin the well-worn conversation with myself. "How could you do that? Where did you go wrong?" In the length of time between strokes, I usually can make a full blown analysis of why the ball ended in the bunker instead of the green. Is it possible to not fall prey to this analysis, judgment, and self-criticism for the so called bad shot? Can we short circuit our tendency to label things as bad or good? Can we postpone dissecting the previous shot? What we need now is to be counter cultural in our view. Polarity or dualistic thinking, good and bad thinking can be put aside. It is possible to keep from dividing things as right and wrong, good and bad. It is possible to step away from a reward/punishment mentality. The difficulty is that from infancy we've lived with this mind set. We receive approval for things that we do right and condemnation for actions that are deemed wrong. We've been carefully trained to be judgmental, to distinguish the good from the bad, to follow the rules, to compare our actions to other similar actions.

But suppose we got rid of the labels? Suppose we determined that all shots are simply there with their own set of challenges? Suppose we stop making comparisons? Once we have hit the ball, where and why it lands is beyond our control. What is done is done. There is an old Dakota Indian saying. "If you find yourself riding a dead horse, don't try to determine why it died; dismount." I think if the Indians played golf they would say, "Don't analyze where the ball has gone. It is now beyond your control. Enjoy the moment."

There is no question that this is difficult. Ben Hogan's advice is certainly good to keep in mind at times like this. "The most important shot in golf is the next one." The difficulty is our inability to think beyond the last shot. This takes practice. It is one thing to recommend it, another to carry it out.

Here is a way to practice beyond the golf

course. Try to go through an entire day without making a negative label, i.e. this way is wrong, that person is not helpful, this choice has negative consequences. When your mind drifts into the land of judgment, be willing to examine where that thought originated. The process of attempting to live a whole day finding positives will enable you to be more positive during the golf game.

One of the ways that I am working on the problem of labels is by learning to say "Yes" and not "No" at the end of each swing. If you start with a No, "No not that again. No, that's not what I meant. No, last week I hit the ball 30 yard further," it's difficult to get to yes. "Yes, this is where I am. Yes, there are many options to get to the green." No is a word that closes things down. Yes is a possibility word. Yes, opens up choices. No is a judgmental word.Yes implies there is more to come.

Eckhart Tolle defines *no* as setting up a negative energy field. What basically happens is that when you label your last shot as a *no*, or bad, accompanied by some negative judgment, and you wish it would go away, it tends to stay with you. What you resist persists.

Another way to look at this is, if you begin with *no*, the game of golf then becomes a problem solving exercise. There is a difference between viewing a shot as a problem or as a teachable moment. You will be amazed at the positive energy and concentration that will happen if you choose to see it as a teachable moment. Once again to quote from Tolle: "Always say *yes* to the present moment. Say *yes* to life and see how suddenly it starts working for you rather than against you. The way to practice *yes* is to go out and play a few holes. Then where ever the ball lands, embrace the next shot as if you had chosen it yourself.

All of this may sound superficial, but these are ways that I choose to experiment as I try to learn to play golf. My learning so far is that what happens on the golf course is not as important as how I react to what has happened.

There is a wonderful story told about Thomas Edison, the inventor. It was said that it took 1000 tries until he produced the light bulb. A reporter asked, "How did it feel to fail 999 times?" "I didn't fail," Edison replied, "I simply found 999 ways how not to make a light bulb."

This is a lesson for those who can't stand failure, who have bought into the culture of success.

Lately, when playing by myself, I am trying this drill. I hit two balls and play the worst of the two. This simulates playing from mistakes.

Richard Rohr, the priest and author has written,

"We grow spiritually much more by doing it wrong, then by doing it right. The demand for the perfect is the greatest enemy of the good."

Golf is a game of mistakes. The important element is what you do with your mistakes. In life there are creative uses of troubles and less creative ways. We can learn from what happens or we can let it overwhelm us. We can decide this is a teachable moment or we can throw up our hands and say, "There goes my perfect day." The only way to fail is to give up and go home, or as many do, when the play is going badly, just continue going through the motions.

We grow more by doing it wrong then by doing it right. The only way I know to learn how to recover from mistakes is by making mistakes. The analogy here is learning to ride a bike. The way to learn balance is by falling off. If you don't try to learn without training wheels or someone holding you, you will never be a bike rider. Trial and error is the way we eventually learn to ride and the same for the game of golf.

The poet, T.S. Eliot said it so well:

We are only undefeated because we keep on trying. For us, there is only the trying. The rest is not our business.

Chapter Four: Letting Go

Now here, you see, it takes all the running you can do to keep in the same place. If you want to get somewhere else, you must run at least twice as fast as that.

Many golf books focus on the "how" question; how to be a better golfer, how to make the drive longer, how to escape from bad lies. The one single question they seem to avoid is why. Why play golf at all? Why do we want to improve? This may seem to be a matter of philosophy. It calls us to speculate on the nature of things, The how questions are more open to rational inquiry. This may be a parallel to life in general. In the how questions we see ourselves as problem solvers. In the why question we see ourselves as residing in the land of speculation and fantasy

One of the more frustrating experiences arises after a ball is hit into the water, or into a difficult patch of rough. Somehow the next few shots turn out to be less than satisfactory. I wonder why bad hits are often sequential? It's often easier to think of how we might have hit a better ball. But the why question is legitimate.

This speculation can lead us into some important insights.

One obvious reason is that we allow ourselves to make an analysis of the previous shot and then try to correct the problem on the next shot. The other day I remember saying to myself, "You lifted your head on the last shot and therefore you topped the ball." This analysis may have been perfectly correct, but in the contemplation of the error, I found myself keeping my neck very tight and not moving my head at all. And sure enough my next swing was a miserable slice.

In business school I can recall a term that was used in a discussion of decision making. The term was "the paralysis of analysis." Overly analyzing a problem, trying to see things from every possible angle, the professor taught, often leads to paralysis, and a failure to act. The same is true in golf. The secret here is not to let the former shot influence the next. Letting go is a skill that is invaluable. If we let go of the former drive, we find that we have much more freedom to choose the right way to address the upcoming shot. Letting go is how to avoid "the paralysis of analysis."

Another reason for hitting a series of bad shots is that the mind set from the previous shot leads us into a negative frame of reference. This is so, particularly if you still carry around a performance orientation. A badly hit ball can quickly affect your feelings of self-worth. The transition from "I hit a bad shot." to I am a bad golfer can happen in an instant. The other day when I hit two balls into the water on two successive holes. I said to myself, "Well you certainly have shown the other three players what a lousy golfer you are." It's difficult to recover after that kind of judgment.

Another problem with successive miss hits is that it can open you to receiving "help" from your partner. Most golfers see themselves as supportive. They are more then ready to give gratuitous advice, particularly when a fellow golfer seems to be in distress. This "help" is usually not what you need. Suggestions of a different club, or trouble with your stance only compounds the problem. The middle of a golf game is no time to get a mini-lesson, or to conduct an experiment. At this point it is your self image that needs help not your swing.

I am reminded that Erickson often quotes a Greek philosopher from the first century; "as a man imagines himself to be, so shall he be, and he is that which he imagines." It may seem almost simplistic to translate that profound statement into, if you feel like a loser, you will end up a loser.

A drill that can give you some perspective on all of

this is to schedule an appointment with disappointment. What you do is choose an entire day being mindful of all your disappointments and frustrations. As you reflect on this day see if you can articulate how you reacted when faced with disappointment and what caused your feelings.

As you become more aware of these feelings, you may observe that your body picks up these signals. Feelings are transmitted through our muscles. A common term in some golf books is muscle memory. This refers to the groove you work through by constantly hitting the golf ball in a certain way. When you feel good about your swing, it indicates that it fits into a groove of your muscles. This may be why golfers are always looking for consistency. It also sets the stage for one of the key tasks. That task is the necessity of being aware of what is happening and of where you are in the midst of your swing.

Let me go one step further and suggest that your posture says a great deal about what will happen next. The way you stride up to the Tee box is a clue to predicting the future. How you hold yourself, your muscle tone, your skeletal structure all point to your self image. Here I would take the advice from Alcoholics Anonymous: "If you can't make it, fake it." Let your imagination take over, and learn to trust that the next shot will be the best you can do at this moment. Doubt and a defeatist attitude can easily contaminate any golf game. The great enemy is fear of bad consequences. The great ally is being able to imagine a desired outcome. One of the secrets to good golf is to believe that your mind is your control tower. The way your mind thinks is the way your game will go. The first step towards good golf is believing you control the tower. As Herbert Dryfus has written, "Mindful self monitoring rather than mindless coping is the paradigm of good golf."

The next step is to put aside feelings of permanence. The problem with many of us is that we basically seek this permanence in all that we do. We hold on to what we have accomplished, with the thought that somehow we can avoid loss or failure, or even death itself. Death focuses on just how impermanent life is. But still our culture denies loss and covers over failure and runs from death. But golf is a game of mistakes. Even though everyone seems to want consistency, most golfers know this will not happen. The game of golf is a game of impermanence.

There is a fable told in several religious circles. It can stand as a reminder when we become discouraged with a series of badly hit balls.

There once was a king who lived in a far off land. The king suffered from depression and mood swings. One day he was ready to give up his kingdom. The next he felt invincible. He realized that neither of these two mind sets was helpful. So he called together all the wise men of the kingdom and charged them to come up with a short sentence which he could say to himself in his alternate moods. The wise men deliberated for many weeks and finally came up with the one sentence the king could use. Say to yourself, they advised ,"This too shall pass."

Facing up to impermanence allows us to handle failure as well as successes without either becoming the last word.   It's possible not to be stuck with what is often seen as the golfer's curse, playing brilliantly one day and like a beginner the next.

One final word that comes from the wisdom of Bob Tuski and Dave Love. In their book, *How to Feel a Real Golf Swing*, they use learning to dance as a metaphor for the game. In learning to dance you are first taught the different steps, where the right and left feet are to go, which foot to start and where to cross over with your feet. Eventually, in order to really dance, you have to let go of these instructions and hear the music. Dancing only happens when you let go of thinking about your feet and go to the rhythm of the music.

The same may be said about golf. Once we know about grip, ball placement, and swing, in order to play golf we need to dismiss these steps and get into a rhythm.

Tuski and Love make the point that golf at its best is not concerned with hitting the ball, but rather is concerned with the rhythm as we swing through the ball. The key is to let go of a focus on the mechanical aspects and re-orient your game. A way to do this is by viewing the golf club as your partner in the dance rather than an instrument for striking the ball. I would also recommend keeping the same sense of rhythm in the back swing as one does in swinging through the ball. I personally hum to myself, "I've got rhythm, I've got rhythm, who can ask for anything more," as I approach the tee.

Chapter Five: The Putting Game

"We had the best of education," the Mock Turtle said. "We had realing and writhing to begin with - and then the different branches of arithmetic ---ambition, distraction, and uglifacation."

"I never heard of uglification;" Alice ventured to say. "What is it?"

The Gryphon lifted both its paws in surprise. "Never heard of uglification," it exclaimed. "You know what to beautify is, I suppose?"

"Yes," said Alice doubtfully. "It means - to - make -- anything prettier."

"Well then," The Gryphon went on, "If you don't know what to uglify is, you are a simpleton."

Some have called putting the game within the game. The other day I looked at my score card and found that I could have shaved four or more strokes by not three or four putting on several greens. Of all the strokes in the game of golf this is the most inviting and the most disturbing at the same time. It seems like child's play to push a white round object six or seven feet into a cup. But it is just at this point that distinguishes the lower from the higher handicapper. My observation is that more has been written about putting and more shown on T.V. than any other part of the game. The putting stroke lends itself to performance feelings as no other. Apart from the initial drive this is the one time where all players stop to watch. It can be a time of embarrassment or of wild exuberance, a time of extensive pain or of blessed healing. "It might have taken five stokes to get on the green, but I did sink that fifteen footer."

I have wondered why the most obvious problem for most average golfers is that the ball comes up short. Direction, understanding the break, reading the green, a proper pendulum swing fall into place, and then the ball seems to have a mind of its own. It stops short of the hole. Is it that we have not looked beyond the cup, or maybe we lifted our head, or twisted the club face? There are suggestions galore to cure these problems. Sometimes they work, but more often than not the tendency is to forget helpful tips when faced with a putt that could easily make the difference between winning and losing.

The one constant to good putting, can be found in

your self-image as a putter. Do you see yourself as an excellent putter? It takes a certain arrogance to be a successful putter. You have to believe that what your doing will place the ball in the cup. Without this belief the ball may land close but not where you meant it to go.

Many times after putting I have asked myself what was going through my mind as I lined up the ball. Too often it was a review of past putts, an awareness of my shot being under scrutiny, and then a review of the score, and what this putt will do to the overall game.

It is hard to think of your self image as a putter when all these thoughts are running through your mind. Many times after completing the stroke we find were not lined up with the hole. Our mind was somewhere else. In putting you fail only when you do not pay attention. It is not failure if you realize you're not in the present moment. Sometimes it is easier to focus your attention on your breathing. It still is important to observe where your attention has wandered. One way to practice this away from the golf course is to sit quietly and attempt to observe yourself. Do you have an itch or an ache somewhere on your body? Observe it. Where does it come from? Try to put it out of your mind. Let other thoughts enter your mind. The reason why this drill is important is that we need to be able to monitor our internal state. We need to practice providing space for more than the initial knee jerk reactions to where we find ourselves. When your mind drifts, examine what has caught your attention.

Golf is not like tennis or any of the other fast moving sports. In games similar to tennis you are almost completely dependent on muscle memory. You don't have the time to think through many options. Tennis players lean heavily on reflex actions in the midst of the game.

Not so with golf. Golf is unique in that there are vast spaces between strokes. If you calculate that the average golfer takes less then a minute to hit the ball, including practice swings etc. and add five strokes per hole. This comes to about 90 minutes where one is actually involved in ball striking activity. The question then is, what happens during the other two or three hours that it takes to play eighteen holes?

Not much has been written about this part of the game, yet it is by far the longest time spent on the course. The so called empty space between shots are where most of our thinking takes place. This time is where we have most control over our restless minds.

There is really no necessity to think of much with the advent of range finders and practice in determining how far one usually hits certain clubs. Most of our trouble starts in the spaces between shots. Our minds are relatively free from thinking about what to do on the next shot Therefore certain mindsets seem to take over. Here are some examples:

The comparing mind: Your partner has made a good drive, and you are on the way to find your less than adequately hit ball. Unconsciously you begin to compare the distance where his landed and your own. This easily leads to a feeling of inadequacy and can morph into envy and general dissatisfaction.

Another one is what I have called the calculating mindset. Here one concentrates upon the score and how future swings will affect your standing. This leads the mind to swing into thinking about results and away from the game itself.

Finally there is the blaming mind. Surely if we had bought a new driver, that errant shot would never have occurred. Or if those rude people had not continued talking, we would have hit it much further. Most of us are experts at the blame game. One reason is that we practice this mind set so much in our everyday life.

The process of putting aside these mind sets as you approach the green is probably the most difficult part of putting. More time is spent on the green, watching other players, lining up your ball, judging distances, then with any other stroke. This gives us an opportunity to introduce extraneous thoughts which can ruin the most well-thought putt.

As far back as 1946 a book on golf came out called *On Learning Golf* by an English professional by the name of Percy Boomer. Boomer recognized the need in golf to replace thinking because he realized that if golf was dependent upon thinking ,it was at the mercy of your mental state. Excitement, depression, anger, almost any emotion could ruin your game.

Consistent golf meant playing independent of mental and physical limitations. He introduced the term *conscious control.* By building up a since of feel in the body, he took the word think and thoughts out of the teaching vocabulary. As true and helpful this might have been, it's also true that we can't dismiss feelings, which are a part of being human.

In a recent newspaper article Jason Day is quoted: "You could have all the tools in the world, but if you really don't want to be there or if there's something off course that's playing on your mind...the game of golf is so mental and if you don't have everything in the right order, it's very difficult to win."

Chapter Six: The Unsatisfactory Score

"I could tell you my adventures---beginning from the morning," said Alice a little timidly, "but it's no use going back to yesterday because I was different then."

I just came home from a round of golf. My score was considerably higher then my handicap. My wife looked at my tight face and said: "Should I dare ask, how did it go?" This innocent question raised some fundamental issues. How do you respond when you have finished with a bad score? A great deal depends upon the way you view yourself.

Are you a victim of the course? Do you recall all the pain, the missed opportunities, the embarrassing score? What do you see as you look into a mirror? Does a victim look back at you? If you are in a victim stance it can affect the rest of your day. You can waste a lot of time and energy trying to put the day behind. It is not easy to deny or erase the pain. Responding as a victim can create a cycle of helplessness. The best a victim can do is to grin and bear it. I happen to notice this advice on a saying found on a Salada Tea bag; "Don't complain about the way a ball bounces, if you are the one who dropped (hit) the ball."

Another way that you might picture yourself is that of a survivor. For this role you can be pleased that you made it through eighteen holes without quitting. You might also admit, in private, that it could have been worse. The best a survivor can do is place the game in a larger context. The former round was simply one blip in a golf career. Somehow this allows you to maintain a future full of hope. A survivor can always say; "Next time things will go better."

The final response is of a Thriver. Here you see the possibilities of drawing learnings from the experience. As Henri Nouwen, the priest and psychologist, has written: "We have to know the darkness to be able to search for the light."

Thriving means that you do not have to deny the score, but somehow you can convert a black mark into a friendly indicator. Admittedly this is not automatic. It takes practice to build a strategy that changes an obvious minus to a plus. One has to go beyond the score. The score is simply a summary. It is not a particularly accurate picture of what actually happened. A Thriver is able to put aside the mental baggage of feeling pain or of feeling like the victim of the god's of golf. A Thriver can reframe the past.

There are many examples of this process in contemporary literature. One of the most memorable is Victor Frankl's account of his concentration camp experience. While most of his fellow inmates lost hope and subsequently died, Frankl occupied his mind thinking about his learnings in the camp. He reframed this horrible experience and made it a source for future lectures.

This reframing can lead a golfer with plenty of material for the next trip to the practice Tee, or if you have a friendly golf professional, it can be the subject of the next lesson.

As we respond to the game by looking at our self image and how we might reframe this time on the golf course, let me add three questions that we might ask ourselves.

First what was your goal for the past round? Most people set goals in order to measure improvement. They use their handicap, or a particular stroke such as the number of putts to determine whether they have improved. I would suggest another way to keep score and measure goals. Rate each hole not on the number of strokes. Rate it as a yardstick of what you learned.

One way to do this is to sit quietly and focus the mind on any hole. Picture what happened. If other thoughts come to mind during this exercise, note them and go back to the hole. Your purpose is to simply observe, no judgments, no intentions of changing, no suggestions of hitting it differently. Your task is to observe the feelings you have about the hit. Try to avoid any label. If you practice this exercise, you will eventually see yourself no longer as a person with a bad score. You will now be an observer of someone with a bad hole.

Another way to score each hole and to view the former round is with a joy evaluation score card. Each hole is evaluated from one to ten. A lower number stands for the hole being a struggle and the higher number stand for the sense of joy one felt as you hit . If you find that most of the holes have lower numbers, you probably have a mind set that results are the most important factor. I have tried to counteract this orientation by repeating a mantra, "If a thing (the game of golf) is worth doing, it's worth doing badly."

The question of how did it go, is misplaced. The more telling question we might ask is what kind of a person are we trying to be? Developing the mind of a *thriver* brings with it a feeling of calm. We are no longer centered on outcome. Instead we can look at our attitude, and what we learned about ourselves. This different focus allows us to appreciate the different meanings we might have discovered on the previous round.

One of the ways to reflect upon bad shots is to ask what really is important. You might learn a great deal if you first answer the question, "As an incident in my total life picture, how would I rate this shot?"

And finally I would ask, have there been any moments of humor? What may happen is that as the score increases, the player becomes more grim. The great problem is that most average golfers keep investing the game with an aura of a crusade and therefore loses the sense of play. Humor helps us keep a sense of proportion. Tension can be relieved by the judicious use of humor. It's important to be able to laugh at the absurdity of hitting a small white ball around the countryside. Somewhere I found these words and wrote them down in my notebook: "Blessed be the golfer who can laugh at himself, for he shall never cease to be amazed." (author unknown)

Chapter Seven: The Nineteenth Hole

"Would you tell me please, which way I ought to go from here?" "That depends a good deal on where you want to go," said the Cheshire Cat.

"I don't much care," said Alice. "Then it doesn't matter which way you go," said the Cat. -- "So long as I get somewhere," Alice added as an explanation.

One of the unwritten traditions of golf is called the 19th hole. Following a round of golf, the players go through a ritual of drinks and conversation. This can be a painful or welcome experience depending on how you have played, your ability to put aside any unpleasant memories, and your communication skills. This is the time when the losers pay up and the winners get to brag. It is also a time to share the ups and downs of the previous game, and can be a time to cement a budding friendship.

For some, it can feel similar to the "show and tell" experienced in early school day years. The times we shared something of interest that had been brought from home.

If one was of a competitive nature, these experiences could be exhilarating or embarrassing. You either brought something that caught the attention of the class or returned to your seat vowing never to volunteer again. The great surprise is how these childish incidents can so easily be transferred to experiences on the golf course.

For others, the 19th hole is a time to garner sympathy. Your drinking companions know what it's like to watch with horror as a ball sails into the water, spoiling a string of pars and a potentially low score day. Everybody at the table can empathize with the trials and tribulations of a golfer's odyssey.

And for still others, this time is an opportunity to learn something more about the game of golf. The ability to reflect on what happened, share some discoveries, and receive some advice can be invaluable. True learning takes place not while we are in the midst of an experience, but when we reflect on these experiences long after the fact. It can be difficult to correct mistakes while on the golf course, but after the game is finished, there is an opening for new possibilities.

This is not to imply the 19th hole is always about golf, nor is it necessarily an instruction time. The conversation usually ranges from the latest gossip to what is happening on the political scene. The important part of the experience is the ability to bond with a group who has just gone through a journey together.

Golf is essentially a communal game. We tend to forget this when the concentration is on self. In one sense there is always an implied opponent. The presence of handicaps assumes that others are playing with you. Handicaps are the way that golf attempts to level the playing field.

Another person's observation can be helpful in increasing your awareness. It is easier to recognize flaws in other people than in yourself. The feedback you receive on the 19th hole can be invaluable. The time spent in this spot is a helpful moment for letting out feeling. This way you need not carry them home with you. And finally, it is a time to practice compassion. No longer need you view the other players as competitors. They are fellow sufferers who feel as you do, the same pain and the same disappointments

Chapter Eight: Anger

And the Caterpillar seemed to be in a very unpleasant state of mind: "Come back," the Caterpillar called after her. "I've something important to say:" This sounded promising. Alice turned and came back again.

"Keep your temper," said the Caterpillar. "Is that all?" said Alice, swallowing her anger as well as she could.

Most golfers have a fair amount of it and they are not very good at handling it. We may deny it, we often swallow it, sometimes we get sick over it. Anger is a common feeling to most golfers.

We have observed how anger can be destructive in situations apart from the golf course. Anger management has risen to new heights in the counseling world. In order to fully enjoy golf however this very common emotion must be recognized and managed.

Anger generates energy. It can be used positively or negatively. The first thing about this energy is that it always is directed at something. The most difficult type of anger is when it is self-directed. It comes about when the anticipated performance is disappointing.

This kind of anger can be very destructive. One's own anger leads into self-punishment, self-doubt, and depression. When this emotion appears, it can be frightening. It arises when we least expect it and seems beyond control. Most of the time we experience anger as an unpleasant feeling. The blood pressure increases, the muscles tense up, and we find ourselves unable to think clearly. When this becomes a problem on the course, we move from simple irritation, to annoyance, and sometimes to a kind of rage that signifies loss of control. We throw a club into the water, we give up, or at least in our minds we leave for home.

Thomas Aquinas once lamented that we lack a word for the virtue of anger. Anger also can cleanse, energize, and help us to focus. In the game of golf, it is possible to channel this emotion in order to make it useful.

Emotions in and of themselves have no moral value. They are neither good nor bad. They are signals alerting us of something to which we should pay attention.

The secret is learning to listen to our emotions instead of obeying them. This calls for a stance of being an observer of oneself. Here are two steps that can easily be taken.

First anger needs to be recognized. Many people miss the early signs until they explode and throw a club or smash a ball.

Second you have to be sensitive to where the feelings originate. Was it the last bad drive? Was it something said by your golfing partner? Or was it something outside of today that you hadn't been able to resolve. Golfers tend to bring a lot of mental baggage to the golf course. It is amazing how last week's argument can influence today's round of golf.

Some people are able to use anger as a safety valve. It helps them reduce tension. Tiger Woods is a case in point. You can see he gets angry, almost to the point of throwing a tantrum but then he puts it behind him on the next shot. The problem, once anger is recognized, is how to keep it from having negative effects on your game. Anger can remain for many a psychic pollutant.

The good news is that anger need not hang over you like a heavy burden. You can recognize the anger without surrendering to it. Once it is acknowledged, it is possible to drop it from your mind. You simply acknowledge its presence and go on with other thoughts. You can either be a spectator to your anger or you take it on as a part of your persona. It's important to keep in mind that there is a difference between feelings of anger which can quickly pass and of becoming an angry person.

There is one further note about anger. Sometimes it can be used as a warning signal that you are losing focus. The discomfort you feel is a signal to stop and come back to the present. Scott Peck reminds us: "Some of our finest moments often occur when we are feeling deeply uncomfortable. It may be in such moments that we are propelled by our discomfort to step out of our ruts." Anger can make you tense, but it can also mark the beginning of a new way to view the game.

Chapter Nine: Negative Outcomes

"But its no use now," thought poor Alice, "to pretend to be two people! Why there's hardly enough of me left to make one respectable person!"

The other day I left the golf course with the vow that I would take up some other sport. To tell the truth I was frustrated, disillusioned, and depressed. Let me try to speak to these three outcomes.

One of the reasons for frustration is that we try to copy other people's strokes. The other day, I was playing with a friend and he suggested I should play like Fred Couples. The problem is that I am not Fred Couples. My body is different, I haven't been playing as long, and my swing is dissimilar. Trying to copy someone else's form is a path that leads to frustration. Many of the books that stress the inner game start with the premise that each person has within himself a natural swing., That natural swing is unique to each person. These authors of the inner game recommend keeping that which is one's own. My swing is my own. It takes into account a bad shoulder, an aging body, and a personality which has been developed through the years. This is not to say there cannot be improvement. But copying another person is not the direction that I would choose. The way to avoid frustration is to start with what you bring to the table. It is your own unique swing, and as you become more aware of what your doing and letting go of any thoughts that you can play like Fred Couples you will progress. This is not to say that one cannot learn from observation. As I watched the smoothness and effortless of Couples' swing, I became aware of my own choppy approach. This opened my awareness of the relationship of my hands to the rest of my body. I began to see the swing through the eyes of the hands. This called for a different perspective on awareness and the feel of the hands. This is sometimes referred to as kinesthetic awareness rather than a focus on the mechanics and form. Tiger Woods said it so well in an interview, "You have to see the shots and feel them through your hands in order to play good golf."

Another reason for my frustration was that I seemed stuck in the endless cycle of playing well on one day and then playing poorly for the next four days. Is it possible improve without going backward? The sense of frustration is that I believe I have learned something and it works one day, and the next four golf rounds seem to indicate that nothing of substance was learned. We long for consistency and we experience the opposite. We take golf lessons and they have the same impact as crash-diet approaches to physical fitness. The results don't last. This is not to say that lessons cannot be helpful. Lessons that increase your awareness of what you are doing and allow you to make your own adjustments are invaluable. It is sometimes difficult to uncover weaknesses by yourself. A neutral observer can be useful. An instructor's practiced eye can also be very helpful.

My next feeling was one of disillusionment. I have found that disillusionment stems from having illusions. When we expect to hit like Tiger Woods, or expect not to have bad shots or expect to have our playing partners remark on how we have improved, these illusions lead to disillusionment. Can you imagine a baseball player expecting to hit a home run every time at bat? Expectations, particularly those that project something unrealistic, are the seed beds for disappointment. It is possible to put aside expectations. This is one of the secrets to playing in the present moment.

On the other hand, how do you measure failure or success in your golf game? You have to expect something from a game, but it may not be defined in the typical way. For high handicappers who may be less competitive, the expectations may include less feelings of a performance, less bruised egos, and more of a willingness to experiment.

The way we look at life also can be a cause of disillusionment. Our assumptions about what will happen on the course can be the beginning of a downward spiral. I get up every morning with a whole set of assumptions. I carry in my head these assumptions about who I am and the way I will play. These assumptions get in the way of seeing what is actually in front of me on the course. I am not advocating denying these thoughts, only suggesting that it is possible to put them aside. I came across a helpful Buddhist saying the other day: "Assumptions bind us to the past, obscure the present, limit our sense of what is possible, and elbow out joy." To play good golf is to keep the joy and ditch the assumptions. As an expert gardener once said to me, "When you see a weed pluck it." When you see an assumption about your game, pluck it.

And finally there is depression. This is one of the more serious emotional problems for the plunkers and plodders. It's a sign that they are taking the game past the golf course. They are no longer playing a game. Golf for some people becomes an all consuming addiction.

Egos are wrapped around scores. The time on the golf course can no longer separated from the rest of the twenty-four. It would seem logical that if you became depressed with golf that you would give it up or take a sabbatical. My observation is just the opposite. Depression and addiction seem to go together. The more depressed one becomes, the more obsessed we are with what has happened. This addiction results in frustration and an inner dissatisfaction that plays over and over in our mind. Golf for some becomes a compulsion and they no longer can view it as a game. We then play it over and over in our minds and this is how the addiction starts. We eat and sleep and even dream about golf. Sometimes we even write about golf. Healing from addiction is possible. This does not mean the depression never existed. It means that the addiction no longer controls our life.

The secret is to develop an undefeated mind, as Dr. Alex Lickerman describes it: "An undefeated mind isn't one that never feels discouraged or despairing. It's one that continues on in spite of it. Possessing an undefeated mind means never forgetting that defeat comes not from failing but from giving up."

Chapter Ten: Acceptance

It'll be no use their putting their heads down and saying, "come up again dear!" I shall only look up and say, "who am I then?" Tell me that first, and then, if I like being that person, I'll come up: if not I'll stay down here till I'm somebody else. Cried Alice, with a sudden burst of tears.

Many hackers and slicers have high hopes and low expectations. We fantasize about the game and then proceed to act out the worst case scenarios'.

In the past five years, the average golfer's handicap has not changed by more than a stroke or two. Can you imagine what that does to a person's self-image?

We live in a success oriented culture. Self-improvement is what its all about in being an American. The unforgivable sin is not working to better oneself. And there stands the average golfer whose handicap remains the same year after year.

Several years ago an important small book came out by Bob Rotella called *Golf is not a Game of*

Perfect. Rotella's premise was that the object of golf was not to make a perfect score. His thesis was welcomed by many average golfers. It represented a breath of freedom for those who were over-achievers.

I would take his premise one step further. The game is not a game of perfect because it is played by imperfect people. There is an old saying: "If an ass goes on a journey, it's not going to come back as a horse."

In our dreams, we imagine we will play like a tour player. We seek perfection or close to it, even when we know it will never happen. The truth about golf is that it is all about limitations. Just as a stream has no possibility of running deep until it finds its banks, so it is with us. Until we face our imperfections, the limits of our game, we haven't much of a chance of lowering our score.

Learning to accept limitations is an important step to growth. Limitations are part of what makes you unique. You may not be strong enough to drive 300 yards, but that doesn't stop you from delighting in recovering after topping a drive. You may not be able to play eighteen holes without making several costly blunders, but that should not bar you from enjoying the day.

There are some wonderful lines from a song by

Leonard Cohen, a popular Canadian song writer: I believe average golfers should hum them to themselves as they contemplate their game: "Ring the bell that can still ring. Forget your perfect offering. There is a crack in everything. That's how the light gets in."

The problem for many plodders and plunkers is that they want to fix the cracks. Somehow we think if we purchase a new club, attempt to follow a new procedure, imitate a well known golfer our handicaps will suddenly lower. My learning is that imperfection is part of who we are. There is no reason to make major changes. Work with what you have. Your swing is unique to you. Certainly you can improve what you have developed, but first you have to learn to accept your game as it is. Eckhart Tolle, again gives us an important saying: "What could be more futile, more insane, than to create inner resistance to what is."

There is a crack in each one of us. For some, golf is a never ending battle to achieve a sense of wholeness, a constant struggle to produce something better than what we did the day before. It becomes a quest for the holy grail rather than a journey of self discovery. When we get caught up in seeking perfection, we miss the point of who we are, imperfect, limited, human beings who are on a journey.

One of the co-conspirators in all this is the handicap system. High handicaps are treated as a mark of shame. Somehow the high numbers expose a sense of imperfection.

Have you ever wondered about the word handicap? We associate the word, outside of the golf world,with an impediment or disadvantage. The handicapped are those who are physically disabled or mentally challenged. We understand in golf that it technically indicates the deferential between the "course rating" and one's score. But for many the word itself can be a source of embarrassment which carries with it different meanings.

Shame is an important factor for the average golfer. We try to soften the feeling by referring to it as a sense of embarrassment. The handicap then for some is a record of bad performances on the golf course. The power of shame can be recognized by feeling of being exposed and vulnerable when handicaps comes up in a conversation. I have labeled it "the wooden leg syndrome." It is my limitation that I try to hide. It is the part of my game that I'm reluctant to reveal. It announces the fact that I am not a serious golfer. It labels me and places me in a category sometimes referred to as a duffer. The important point to keep in mind is that one's handicap is not a measure of self-worth

Learning to accept one's imperfection is the beginning of wisdom for the average golfer. Martin Luther King Jr. in one of his early speeches said, "Only those who can accept the darkness can appreciate the light." Denying our imperfection is somehow disowning oneself. Handicaps are not signs of failure, only marks of boundaries. Be thankful for the cracks. Here is where we learn about life.

A friend observed that Americans are more addicted to perfection than other nations. This can be seen in the way we design our golf courses as opposed to Scottish or European courses. American designers value length and usually design courses to be much flatter leading to small, and also flat greens. Scottish and European golf courses were laid out in a different way. They value strategic intelligence over categories of perfection in one's swing. Their courses often have deep bunkers placed directly in the line of play forcing something less than a perfect shot. They are laid out in such a way as to keep players from making par. For example, bunkers were put where you would more naturally hit, right in the middle. American courses use bunkers to penalize the bad shot. They are usually found on the side of the green. My friend speculated that this difference had to do with the cultural trait, Although we know we will never reach perfection, we constantly try to reach that goal. We seek constantly to have the perfect family, the perfect job, and the perfect golf game. This cultural desire, he said, has influenced the golf designers. Golf courses are laid out in such a way that it is possible to better your score by becoming a more skillful ball hitter and this easily becomes the main objective. Less strokes rather than enjoying the walk is what American courses seem to be saying.

One of the problems that we may have inherited from this cultural bias toward perfection is that we make excessive demands upon ourselves. This perfectionist ethic is shared by many golfers. Here are five questions you might ask yourself, if you wonder whether you are a perfectionist.

1. When you make a mistake, do you find it hard to forget?

2. Do you often find yourself saying; If I had only done----?

3. Do you constantly compare your game to others?

4. Do you constantly tell yourself to try harder?

5. Do you find it hard to admit your weaknesses?

If you said yes to any of these five questions, you might be classified as a perfectionist. This is not to say standards ought not to be kept up. The test simply emphasizes how the culture has ensnared all of us in a no win game. Perfection is not the goal in golf. Enjoyment, finding meanings, connecting with nature and other people, are more important golf objectives.

It is also necessary to acknowledge that perfectionism is very much a part of the air we breath. To completely eliminate thoughts of perfection is to be radically counter intuitive. There is within all of us that tiny voice saying, do better, try harder, winning is everything.

To deny this cultural pressure is to make it stronger. The better strategy is to let it speak. The thought that tells us we must be perfect is just one thought among many that come to mind as we play the game. Listen to that voice but do not give it more authority then it deserves.

Let me end this chapter with a story. It's not about golf, but certainly makes the point regarding imperfection.

The Vice President of a large company was greatly admired for his energy and drive, but he suffered one embarrassing weakness. Each time he entered the

President's office to make his weekly report, he would wet his pants. The kindly President advised him to see a urologist, at company expense.

The following week he appeared before the President and his pants were again wet. "Didn't you see the urologist?" asked the President. "No, he was out," said the nervous executive. "I saw a psychiatrist instead, and I'm cured. I no longer feel embarrassed."

The bad news is that we often play golf to have our views of our culture confirmed. (If it's cracked we ought to find a way to put it back together.) The good news in all this is that we can learn to accept the cracks for this isn't a game of perfect. (All our imperfections need not be fixed.)

Ring the bell that can be rung, forget perfection. There are cracks in everything, that's how the light gets in.

Chapter Eleven: In The Zone

Oh how I wish I could shut up like a telescope. I think I could if only I knew how to begin. For you see so many out of the way things had happened lately that Alice had began to think that very few things indeed were really possible.

Playing in the Zone is a favorite expression for golfers. Rarely is it explained. And rarely does it happen. In the Zone is an expression common to most sports. It usually refers to a magical moment when you can't miss, when everything comes together, when you're at that peak performance time. Even the over the hill and the under average types are able to have glimpses of this phenomenon, albeit on rare occasions. This is an important state of mind, for when you're in the Zone the game of golf is at its most satisfactory and your playing at your best.

Let's first approach the subject from the negative standpoint. How do you know when your not in the Zone? The first thing is your aware that your not fully present. Some have described this state as being half awake, a condition where you lose focus. Where you give yourself certain messages, such as slow the swing, or don't raise your head. Then you find that by the time you're half way through your swing, you have forgotten what you intended to do. Or your mind is somewhere else. Or your game is tied up with your ego and you are just concentrating on your performance. The list can be quite long, and all of these feelings are signs that you are not in the Zone. Or we might say, you are playing your normal game.

The great problem for most of us is that we have what the Buddhists refer to as "a monkey mind." Our mind is easily distracted like a monkey who can not sit still. The mind jumps from one place to another. When you have a monkey mind emotions like fear, anger, doubt and despair pull you from place to place. You are unaware of what is in front of you.

The two most common demons which block our being in the zone are anticipation of the future and memories of the past.

Relinquishing these preconceptions and expectations, putting aside these thoughts are probably the most difficult tasks for any golfer. It calls for regular practice in monitoring our restless minds and then a commitment to a different mind set. This is often referred to as playing in the zone. In its most simple terms, we are being alert to the present. This demands us to look for what is rather than looking for something that yet may be.

As the Buddhist teachers would say; "The past is gone. The future is not here. If we go back to the present moment, we can be in touch with our experience as it unfolds."

Having approached the subject from a negative, stance let's look at some of the ways that we might recognize when we are in the Zone, if only for a few moments.

The first sign of being in the Zone is the feeling of being in the *now*. You can put aside the monkey mind and focus entirely on the present moment. Some have described the feeling as when my nerves are calm, my body feels loose, and I am enjoying the moment. Others have said, it's when I stop thinking of how to hit the ball. And still others have described it as a psychological and physiological state of flow where we are immersed in an activity so completely that self-consciousness is lost and the only focus is the task at hand. In the ancient tradition, living in the present moment was called the "Nunc Eternum"-- The eternal *now*. This is a sense of awareness that early mystics described as a gift from

God. It was only open to those on a spiritual quest. Maybe seeking the Zone on the golf course could be construed as a golfers spiritual quest?

In golf the Zone is described as all your senses, your entire being is directed to what's in front of you, the ball. It's as if you have been able to blank out the rest of the world. The past is gone and the future has no hold, you are completely in the *now*.

Eckhart Tolle writes: " Most of us are never fully present in the *now* because unconsciously we are either living in the past or thinking about the future, believing that the next moment must be more important than this one. But then you will miss your whole life which is never *not now*." My own experience is that I quickly fall out of this Zone when I begin thinking of the score, or being aware of what other golfers are doing, or I start to be impatient, or I begin to think about my form.

All of this advice is more about perceptions than thoughts. It calls for insight, a reconditioning of our minds, in order to stay in the present. What we find time and time again is that we really are our own worst enemy. We usually see the problems of golf as being "out there" and not "in here." If playing in the zone is your goal, the good news is that it is possible to transform the way your mind works. A good way to start is by saying yes to whatever comes your way. This is a way to start, but always remember you can not acquire a formula for being in the zone, instead you fall into it as a gift from whatever golf gods you happen to believe in.

Having said this, probably the most important learning regarding the Zone is that you cannot engineer it. We can say to ourselves "Today I will play in the zone." But experience tells us that it doesn't happen that way. Playing in the Zone is more analogous to finding a sense of flow rather then following a set pattern.

I wish I knew how to miraculously be in the Zone at any given time. I'm sure that I'd be at least the club champion. All I can point to is that when we're in the Zone, everything seems to work. I have been helped by going through an exercise of becoming aware of colors and shapes. Erickson pointed out to his patients how every blade of grass is a different shade. He also had them describe the shape of trees or buildings. This was not done to help their golf game, but simply as a preliminary exercise to move people into the *now*. I have found this as well as some deep breathing exercises prepare me to move into the present moment. The trick is to experiment and find out what works.

The zone is a practice to be developed. It is not a miracle that happens every so often. Playing in the zone calls for a particular kind of awareness, a deliberate way of paying attention, a putting aside thoughts of the past or of the future. What often blocks us is that we feel we already know what will happen. What we need is a beginners mind. Playing in the zone is not about achieving results. It's about being in the present moment. Once you are in the Zone you no longer have to push because you are already there.

Letting go, as described in an earlier chapter, is more to the point than any formula that we might dream up

Bhagwahn Shrec Rejneesh, the Indian mystic, in *The Book of Secrets* describes this technique as seeing things as if it were for the first time. He claims that we get in the habit of not seeing familiar situations. We see things but we do not focus. "Look freshly," he says, "as if for the first time and your eyes will be open." Who knows, you might find yourself in the Zone?

Chapter Twelve: Making Friends with the Enemy

Alice said, "This is impossible." The Mad Hatter replied, "Only if you believe it........Why sometimes, I've believed as many as six impossible things before breakfast."

The question was asked, in a recent survey of two thousand golfers, "Do you enjoy a round of golf?" Sixty percent of the respondents answered: Never. When this statistic was shared, someone observed, "They seem to be spending their hard earned money doing something that makes them miserable."

The feelings generated by a round of golf for the sixty percent group are often fear, shame, and a sense of isolation. Is it any wonder for some the game is more about work than play, more about performance than learning, more about achievement than self-knowledge, more about winning than relaxation.

We often face the course as if we were a general with a variety of weapons to conquer the enemy. At the conclusion of the battle a grade is received on how many obstacles we avoided or surmounted.

But what would happen if we welcomed those so called obstacles.?What would happen if we greeted them as old friends, opportunities to practice certain strokes, chances to experiment with different clubs? Or what would happen if we began to appreciate the fact the course was designed with such things as miniature lakes to break up the monotony of fairways, and bunkers to make the game more challenging?

Then there is the business of shame. So much of a golf game can be filled with moments of self-directed anger, feelings of shame, and occasions of disappointment at the topped ball, the shot that dribbles into the water, the mighty drive that lands out of bounds.

To make the golf course a friend we have to still the voices in our head. You cannot completely erase these voices, but you can lessen their power by concentrating on affirming the life giving aspects of the game. And doing your level best to remain in the *now*.

Golf can teach us a great deal about patience and forgiveness. The most difficult road block to forgiveness is learning to forgive oneself. It is difficult to forgive oneself for the ill-conceived play that often accompanies the average golfer. Our culture has taught us that forgiveness is something you earn, it isn't freely given. For those who live by this understanding, forgiveness comes by making an outstanding next shot. Can a wining next shot really be the ticket to forgiveness? This understanding puts a huge pressure on the next stroke and usually guarantees a miss hit. But without this interpretation how else could you earn forgiveness?

Another piece of advice is to simply forget the former mistake. Most of us know from experience the more you attempt to forget a past bad choice, the more it sticks in your mind. Golfers have a tendency to remember the painful and forget the occasional good shots.

But suppose forgiveness means seeing yourself in a different light. Changing the inner narrative that broadcasts "You are a lousy golfer," to seeing yourself as a potential good golfer or even as a work in progress. Then forgiveness would mean throwing away the score and relating to oneself in a new way.

Henri Nouwen, one of my spiritual guides, suggests that along with forgiveness we cultivate a sense of patiently waiting. "The word *patience* means the willingness to stay where you are and live the situation to its fullest in the belief that something hidden would manifest itself to us."

It is my belief that hidden behind every golfer is an image of a good golfer. I call this the golfer behind the golfer. We're never fully that person, but every now and then we do see glimpses. If we wait patiently and keep our eyes open for a brief moment there he is. And that for many is enough to keep us playing the game.

When you play golf, you are essentially alone. No matter how many people who play with you, ultimately you are competing against yourself or playing against the course. The is hard for most people to grasp. We live in a society that is built upon competition. We play games to gain an advantage over someone else. It is hard to adjust to doing something for the sake of doing This sense of isolation can result in a feeling of disequilibrium and result in the search for outside help. Someone once described a golfer as a man riding an ox, and still looking all around for an ox. The ox represents the outside rescue, yet within us lies the real answers to our golf game. This sense of isolation can result in our inability to appreciate that which is inside of ourselves.

In order to fully appreciate golf to its fullest, one needs the mind of an artist. Certainly, we all see trees and grass, sunlight and birds, bushes and flowers but if you don't see it with the eyes of an artist, you will miss seeing the lovely shapes of the trees, the multi colors of the grass growing beneath your feet, the birds calling to each other, the bushes spreading their arms and the flowers blooming even in the midst of summer. It is only with the eyes of an artist that you can sense the abundance before you, and be overwhelmed with gratitude at being at one with all you survey. No longer need you be isolated for all of nature calls you to embrace the game the way an artist would contemplate a magnificent scene he was about to paint.

This is both philosophically and practically difficult to imagine. We have been taught to use nature. Even the Bible seems to imply that we are somewhat above nature, as Genesis states, "We are to have dominion over the earth." (Geneses 1:28)

To seek to be *one* with nature calls for a change. It is a radical departure in our theology as well as having implications for the way we play golf. It asks us to let go of that person we have always known and realize you are something other than you thought you were. You thought you were the center of your world, the major performer of your life. You are now being asked to see yourself as simply a part of the overall game, part of what is.

As one writer has said: "You thought you were the

dancer. You now are asked to experience yourself as a part of the dance." This calls for a major change of our perception of the game of golf.

Many of us are slow learners. We may not be there yet, but that does not negate our starting And we can begin by making friends with ourselves, the course, and the game we call golf.

As I prepare to play another round, the words of Eckhart Tolle echo through my mind.

Whatever the present moment contains

Accept it as if you had chosen it.

Always work with it and not against it.

Make it your friend and ally and not your enemy.

This will miraculously transform your life.

Chapter Thirteen: The Last Chapter

"But I don't want to go among mad people," Alice remarked.

"Oh you can't help that," said the Cat. "Were all mad here." "How do you know I'm mad," said Alice? "You must be," said the Cat, "or you wouldn't have come here."

I would offer you this story, to those of you who have taken this journey with me and are still able to watch the ball sail out of bounds, plunk in the water, buried in the sand and still smile and see the beauty of the day It is a child's story, but for those who have gone on this odyssey you might identify with the principal character. The author of the story which I have adapted with apologies, is Shel Silverstein, and he called his story, "The Missing Piece."

The principal character is a partially round figure. In your mind just draw a round circle. I'm sorry that you can not actually see a picture. You will have to use your imagination. The only problem is this figure has a missing piece. Take out a slice from the circle you have drawn in your mind. This makes our hero very anxious. He sees other pieces rolling along way ahead of him. As this piece rolls along, in a bumpy and unsteady way it sings a little song.

Oh, I'm looking for my missing piece,

I'm looking for my missing piece.

Hi - dee --ho, here I go

Looking for my missing piece.

Because it was missing a piece it could not role very fast or straight. But it was able to smell the flowers and appreciate the countryside.

One day, it spied a piece by the side of the road. It seemed to fit, and so our hero began to sing.

I've found my missing piece

I've found my missing piece

so, grease my knees, and fleece my bees

I've found my ---

"Wait a minute said the missing piece, the one that had been found at long last. Before you go greasing your knees and fleecing your bees. I am not your piece. I am someone else's piece.

"Oh our hero," said sadly. I am sorry to have

bothered you," and on it slowly rolled.

A short time later he found another piece, but after many tries, he had to put it down. It was too big and didn't fit. In the book that this was taken from, there are many pictures and stories that go with his adventures in trying to find the missing piece.

Finally, he came upon another piece that seemed just right. "Are you anybody's missing piece," he asked? "Not that I know of," responded the piece. "Well, maybe you want to be your own piece?"

"I can be someone's and still be my own." "Well let's try it." Sure enough they fit, and because of the fit our hero rolled so fast he couldn't stop to smell the flowers. And when he tried to sing it sounded like this:

I've frown my mizzen geez,

uf vron my mitzen brees

So kees my meas

An bleez my drees

Now that it was complete, it couldn't sing at all. He didn't even enjoy rolling in the countryside. So he stopped and set the piece down and slowly bumpily rolled away. As it rolled, it seemed to be filling in the missing parts from within himself. And it began to sing.

I no longer am looking for my missing piece.

So Hi -- Dee -- Ho, here I go

Grease my knees, and fleese my bees

I've found within me, my missing piece.

The last picture in the story book is of our hero with a butterfly perched on its top with still parts of his piece missing. But--and this is important--it is happily rolling along.

This child's story has the power to speak to many of us. For some, the message is simply be careful about what you hope for. It may not be what you need. For others it's a story reminding us to accept where we are. And for still others it suggests that you need not look outside yourself for ways to play the game. The secret is that we don't make ourselves into a better golfer. We discover the golfer within ourselves. Nothing need be changed, but everything can be different. The good news is that you have within yourself the oil that greases the wheel of better golf. It might take you a month, a year, or a lifetime to learn to play with joy. Just begin,and each time begin again . And don't forget to smell the flowers, rejoice at the grass beneath your feet, be thankful for the sun and the clouds, delight in the wind as it caresses your face. And remember this is a game to be enjoyed.

In the end three things matter most. How long you were able to stay in the present. How deeply did you let go. And how fully did you enjoy your time on the course.

Bibliography

Alice in Wonderland Lewis Carroll, edited by Donald Gray

Falling Upward, Richard Rohr

Extraordinary Golf, Fred Shoemaker

The Book of Secrets, Bhagwan Shree Rajneesh

The Power of Now, Eckhart Tolle

My voice will go with you," Sidney Rosen (The teachable tales of Milton Erickson)

From Death Camp to Existentialism, Victor Frankl

The Missing Piece, Shel Siverstein

The Spirituality of Imperfection, Ernest Kurtz and Katherine Ketcham,

Restoring Hope, Robert Voyle

Uncommon Therapy, Jay Haley (*The Psychiatric Techniques of Milton H. Erickson*)

Golf is not a Game of Perfect, Bob Ruffino

Discernment, Henri Nouwen

Anthem, Leonard Cohen

An Undefeated Mind, Alex Lickerman

On Learning Golf, Percy Boomer

Acknowledgements

There are many people to thank for this book. Several friends have read drafts and been good enough to make comments, particularly Nelson Reid and Chotsie Blank. The original idea for the book came in the midst of a lesson with Chris Olseth, who graciously loaned me several books from his library. Then I was initially helped and supported by Michael Lach who introduced me to the work of Fred Shoemaker.

Most of all, I want to thank my long suffering wife, Peggy. Although not a golfer her editing skills and suggestions were invaluable.

As in several other of my books, this publication could not have happened without Dr. James Kelley's excellent editorial advice and publishing expertise.

I also want to acknowledge the help and good instructions I have received from Nick DeKock, Willy Gathrum, Chris Olseth, and Curtis Hayden. Their patience and advice have been extremely helpful. My lack of skill is not that they haven't tried.And finally, I want to thank my golfing friends at Marrakesh Country Club for putting up with a student golfer as he tries to learn to play the game.

Roger Douglas

Palm Desert 2015

Made in the USA
Middletown, DE
25 October 2022

13484840R00057